K

Comprehension Strategy Assessment

CSA

Second Edition

Levels A–E/1–8

Grade **K**

BENCHMARK EDUCATION COMPANY

Benchmark Education Company
145 Huguenot Street • New Rochelle, NY • 10801

Printed in Guangzhou, China. 4401/0315/CA21401924

ISBN: 978-1-4900-6834-3
For ordering information, call Toll-Free 1-877-236-2465 or visit our Web site at www.benchmarkeducation.com.

Table of Contents

This book provides assessments for measuring a child's grasp of comprehension strategies in reading and listening. At the Kindergarten/Emergent level, all assessments are intended to be read aloud. Children listen to stories and passages read aloud and then answer questions. Information from these assessments can be used to support instruction.

This book contains three types of assessments:

- The **Pretest** is designed to assess a child's comprehension strategies at the beginning of the school year. It provides five short reading passages, both fiction and nonfiction, with a total of sixteen multiple-choice items. Information from the Pretest can be used to help plan instruction, make curriculum decisions, and select reading materials to match a child's needs. Pretest scores can also be used as baseline data for evaluating a child's progress from the beginning of the school year to the end.

- **Ongoing Comprehension Strategy Assessments** are focused, one-page assessments to be administered periodically during the school year. Each assessment has a reading passage and two test items to measure one specific strategy. There are two assessments per strategy, and they are intended to be used to monitor a child's progress. The assessments may be administered after completing instruction in particular strategies, or they may be administered at other appropriate times, such as the end of a teaching unit.

- The Midyear and Posttest are parallel to the Pretest. They contain the same number of reading passages and items as the Pretest, and test the same strategies. The **Midyear Test** can be administered as a formulative assessment. The results can be used to adjust instruction to improve student learning. The **Posttest** is designed to be administered at the end of the school year as a final evaluation of a child's progress in comparison to their performance at the beginning of the year.

The next few pages in this book provide directions for administering and scoring the assessments and using the assessment results. Following the general directions are four sections: Pretest, Ongoing Assessments, Midyear Test, and Posttest. Specific directions for administering each assessment and the relevant answer keys can be found at the beginning of each section. Scoring Charts for scoring the assessments and recording results can be found on pages 94–96.

DIRECTIONS FOR ADMINISTERING AND SCORING ASSESSMENTS

All of the assessments in this book may be administered to children individually or in groups. We recommend administering the Pretest, Midyear Test, and Posttest to small groups of four or five children at the same time. The Ongoing Comprehension Strategy Assessments may be administered in the same way, or they may be administered individually to different children at different times. Detailed guidelines for administering and scoring each type of assessment are presented below.

GUIDELINES FOR USING THE PRETEST

The Pretest is eight pages long. It includes five short passages and a total of sixteen multiple-choice questions. These sixteen items measure four "clusters" of strategies and skills (as listed on the Scoring Chart, page 94) with four items per cluster. Each cluster has two or three strategies grouped by similarities. For example, "Compare and Contrast" and "Identify Sequence of Events" are grouped together in one cluster because they involve similar thinking skills (determining how ideas or events are related). Each cluster has been labeled with a title that reflects the key thinking skill, such as "Relating Ideas" Plan for about 20 minutes to administer the Pretest, but allow more time if needed. Children should be allowed to finish answering every question. Depending on the children and your situation, you may want to administer the Pretest in two parts in different sittings. If children have too much difficulty with this kind of assessment, especially at the beginning of the year, you may want to discontinue the assessment and try again at a later time.

To Administer the Pretest:

1. Make a copy of the test for each child.

2. Write the child's name and the date at the top of each test page.

3. Give each child a crayon, pencil, or marker for circling answers.

4. Read the directions and the sample item on the first page and make sure children understand what to do.

5. Instruct children to listen as you read each passage and the questions.

6. For each question, instruct children to choose the best answer and draw a circle around the picture.

7. When children have finished, collect the tests.

To Score the Pretest:

1. Make a copy of the Individual Pretest Scoring Chart (see page 94) for each child.

2. Refer to the Pretest Answer Key on page 15.

3. Mark each question correct or incorrect on the test page.

4. To find the total test score, count the number of items answered correctly.

5. Within each cluster, use the Individual Pretest Scoring Chart. Circle the number of each item answered correctly. The item numbers are organized by clusters of tested skills.

6. For each cluster on the scoring chart, add the number of items answered correctly (for example, 3 of 4). Write the number correct in the right-hand column under Pretest.

Using the Results:

1. Use the results of the Pretest to determine each child's current level of reading/ listening comprehension, as well as his or her proficiencies in the strategies being tested.

2. As explained above, the items in the Pretest measure strategies in particular clusters. A child's score on a particular cluster can pinpoint specific instructional needs. A child who answers correctly fewer than 3 of the 4 items in each cluster may need focused instructional attention on those particular strategies.

3. Plotting scores on the Individual Scoring Chart and Group Pretest/Midyear Test/ Posttest Comparison provides a handy reference for monitoring a child's growth and development. Such information can be used to identify the skills and strategies to be reinforced for a whole group, small group, or individual.

4. Store the Scoring Charts for the Pretest/Midyear Test/Posttest in an appropriate location for referral during the school year, and for end-of-year comparison of the Pretest and Posttest scores.

GUIDELINES FOR USING THE ONGOING COMPREHENSION STRATEGY ASSESSMENTS

In this program, Kindergarten/Emergent covers ten comprehension strategies. In this book you will find two assessments for each strategy. The assessments are numbered 1–20, and each assessment is one page.

The purpose of these assessments is to determine how well a child has learned each strategy. You may want to administer the two strategy-based assessments at set times of the year (such as during the second and third quarters), or you can administer an assessment for a specific strategy just after teaching the strategy in the classroom. Although the assessments are numbered sequentially 1 through 20, they do not need to be administered in any set order. You may choose to assess any strategy in whatever order you teach them.

Each Ongoing Comprehension Strategy Assessment consists of a short reading passage and two questions. The text of the reading passage and the actual questions appear only in the teacher directions. They are intended to be read aloud. The child's test page has a title and an illustration related to the passage, followed by the answer choices for two multiple-choice items. Each answer choice is a picture of some kind.

Plan for about 10 minutes to administer an Ongoing Comprehension Strategy Assessment, but allow more time if needed.

To Administer an Ongoing Assessment:

1. Make a copy of the assessment for each child.

2. Instruct the child to write his or her name and the date at the top of each test page (or write this information for the child if needed).

3. Give the child a crayon, pencil, or marker for circling answers.

4. Instruct children to listen as you read the passage and the questions.

5. For each question, instruct children to choose the best answer and draw a circle around the picture.

To Score an Ongoing Assessment:

1. Refer to the appropriate Answer Key (on pages 26–27). The answer key gives the correct response for each question.

2. Mark each question correct or incorrect on the test page.

3. To find the total score, count the number of items answered correctly.

Using the Results:

1. Use the results of the Ongoing Assessment to evaluate each child's understanding of the tested strategy or skill.

2. A child who understands and applies a given strategy should answer both items correctly—or 3 out of 4 questions on the two assessments combined. A child who answers only one or none of the items correctly may need additional instruction on a particular strategy.

3. Use the Ongoing Strategy Assessment Record to keep track of a child's scores on the assessments during the school year. The record provides space for writing the score on each of the two strategy assessments (and/or for both assessments combined) and for noting comments relevant to a child's progress in learning a particular strategy.

GUIDELINES FOR USING THE MIDYEAR AND POSTTESTS

The Midyear and Posttests contain the same number of reading passages and items as the Pretest, and should be administered and scored in the same way. The items on the tests measure the same skills as the Pretest with the same number of items in each skill cluster. Thus, the children's scores on the three tests can be compared using the Group Pretest/Midyear Test/Posttest Comparison Chart on page 97.

Use the results of the Midyear Test to pinpoint specific instructional needs. A child who answers two or more items in a skill cluster incorrectly may need focused instructional attention on those particular comprehension strategies.

Use the results of the Posttest to determine each child's current level of reading/listening comprehension, as well as his or her proficiencies in the strategies being tested. Compare each child's scores on the Pretest and Posttest—and on each strategy cluster within the tests—to evaluate the child's progress since the beginning of the year.

COMPREHENSION STRATEGY ASSESSMENTS ONLINE

The Comprehension Strategy Assessments are also available online. The online tests can be administered on any device, including desktop computers, laptops, and tablets. They give children valuable experience with online testing, and offer teachers robust data-driven assessment with reporting by classroom, grade, school, and district.

DIRECTIONS FOR ADMINISTERING THE PRETEST

This section provides specific directions for administering the Pretest to one or more children. When you are ready to begin, read through the sample question and instruct children to mark their answers. Hold up a copy of the test page with the answer circled as a model to show what it looks like. Then proceed with the Pretest by reading the passages and items. Pause after each question to allow time for children to mark their answers. If at any time children seem to be having great difficulty with this kind of testing, discontinue the assessment and try again at another time.

To begin, be sure children have the first page of the Pretest in front of them. Read aloud the directions printed in **bold** type.

Today I am going to read some stories. I will ask you some questions about each story. Listen carefully and follow along as I read. Then answer each question. First we will read a practice question.

Sample

I am going to read a sentence about a girl named Emma. Then I am going to ask a question. Listen to this sentence:

Emma has a new kite with a long tail.

Now put your finger on the row where you see the little toy car. Look at the pictures. What does Emma have? Does she have a flower . . . a key . . . or a kite? Draw a circle around the picture that shows what Emma has. (Pause.) You should have made a circle around the kite. That is the correct answer.

Answer any questions that children may have. When children are ready, administer the test by reading these directions. Check to make sure children are on the correct page.

Now I am going to read you a story about Manny the Elephant. Then I will ask you two questions about the story. Listen carefully.

> One day, Manny the Elephant is eating hay in his house. He feels sad. "No one comes to see me," thinks Manny. Then he hears a noise. He walks out the door of his house and looks through the bars. Five children are waiting for him. They clap and cheer when he comes out. "Finally," thinks Manny. "I have some visitors!"

1. **Put your finger on the row where you see the shoe. Now look at the pictures. In this story, where is Manny? Is he in the forest . . . in the zoo . . . or in a barn? Draw a circle around the picture that shows where Manny is.**

2. **Move down to the next row where you see the apple. Now look at the pictures. How does Manny feel when he is eating hay? Does he feel sad . . . angry . . . or happy? Draw a circle around the picture that shows how Manny feels when he is eating hay.**

Tell children to turn to the next page.

Now I am going to read a story about something you can make.

> You can make a parachute for your favorite toy person. It's easy to do. All you need is a paper napkin and four pieces of string. First, open up the napkin. Next, tie one string to each corner of the napkin. Then, tie all four strings to your toy. Now your toy has a parachute! You can drop your toy. It will float to the floor.

3. **Put your finger on the first row where you see the star. Now look at the pictures. What should you do first? Should you tie the threads on the napkin . . . place the napkin on a table . . . or open the napkin? Draw a circle around the picture that shows what you should do first.**

4. **Move down to the next row where you see the dog. Now look at the pictures. If you follow these directions, what do you have when you finish? Draw a circle around the picture that shows what you have when you finish.**

Tell children to turn to the next page.

Now I am going to read a story about a girl named Kayla. Then I will ask four questions about the story. Listen carefully.

> On Friday, Kayla made a paper bluebird at school. It had paper wings. It was colored blue. After school, Kayla brought the bluebird home and showed it to her mom. Kayla and her mom hung the bluebird over her bed on a string. That night, Kayla brushed her teeth and climbed into bed. She looked up at the bluebird and smiled. It was so pretty! Then Mom turned off the light, and Kayla closed her eyes.

5. **Put your finger on the row where you see the sun. Now look at the pictures. In this story, what will happen next? Will Kayla show the bird to her mom . . . fly like a bird . . . or go to sleep? Draw a circle around the picture that shows what will happen next.**

6. **Move down to the next row where you see the umbrella. Now look at the pictures. Where did Kayla get the bluebird? Did she get it from a nest . . . at school . . . or at the store? Draw a circle around the picture that shows where Kayla got the bluebird.**

Tell children to turn to the next page.

7. **Put your finger on the row where you see the teddy bear. Now look at the pictures. What does Kayla do just before she goes to bed? Does she make a bird . . . brush her teeth . . . or read a book? Draw a circle around the picture that shows what Kayla does just before she goes to bed.**

8. **Move down to the next row where you see the house. Now look at the pictures. How does Kayla feel when she goes to bed? Does she feel happy . . . surprised . . . or sad? Draw a circle around the picture that shows how Kayla feels when she goes to bed.**

Tell children to turn to the next page.

Now I am going to read a story about a kind of food. Then I will ask four questions about the story. Listen carefully.

> Farmers grow a lot of corn. Ears of corn grow on tall plants. Farmers grow corn because it has many uses. Corn is a good food for farm animals. Pigs and cows like to eat corn. It is a good food for people, too. People like to eat sweet corn on the cob. Corn is used to make cereal. It is used to make bread, tortillas, and muffins. It is used to make popcorn and corn oil. Corn is used for many things.

9. Put your finger on the row where you see the fish. Now look at the pictures. What is this story mostly about? Is it about pigs . . . farmers . . . or corn? Draw a circle around the picture that shows what the story is mostly about.

10. Move down to the next row where you see the cat. Now look at the pictures. Which animal likes to eat corn? Is it a dog . . . a cow . . . or a horse? Draw a circle around the picture of an animal that likes to eat corn.

Tell children to turn to the next page.

11. Put your finger on the row where you see the moon. Now look at the pictures. Some farmers grow corn because it can be used to make what? Can it be used to make cereal . . . ice cream . . . or mashed potatoes? Draw a circle around the picture of something that is made from corn.

12. Move down to the next row where you see the ball. Now look at the pictures. Which picture shows a kind of corn you would see at a movie theater? Draw a circle around the picture that shows a kind of corn you see at a movie theater.

Tell children to turn to the next page.

Now I am going to read a story about bees and ants. Then I will ask four questions about the story. Listen carefully.

Bees and ants are fascinating. They are alike in some ways. Both bees and ants are insects. They have six legs. All bees have wings and can fly. Most ants do not have wings. They stay on the ground. Bees live in a hive, and they can sting. Ants live in a nest under the ground, and they can bite. Both bees and ants live in large groups and work together. Bees have a queen, and ants do, too. The worker bees bring food for the queen. Worker ants bring food for their queen, too.

13. **Put your finger on the row where you see the sock. Now look at the pictures. What can bees do that most ants cannot do? Can bees dig under the ground . . . bite your toe . . . or fly in the air? Draw a circle around the picture of something that bees can do but ants cannot.**

14. **Move down to the next row where you see the paintbrush. Now look at the pictures. What do both bees and ants have? Is it a hive . . . a queen . . . or an underground nest? Draw a circle around the picture of something both bees and ants have.**

Tell children to turn to the next page.

15. **Put your finger on the row where you see the book. Now look at the pictures. You can tell from this story that all insects have what? Do all insects have teeth . . . stingers . . . or six legs? Draw a circle around the picture of something that all insects have.**

16. **Move down to the next row where you see the truck. Now look at the pictures. Which picture shows something you learned about in this story? Draw a circle around the picture that shows something you learned about in the story.**

(End of Pretest)

1. in the zoo (2nd picture)
2. sad (1st picture)
3. open the napkin (3rd picture)
4. toy man with parachute (2nd picture)
5. go to sleep (3rd picture)
6. at school (2nd picture)
7. brush her teeth (2nd picture)
8. happy (1st picture)
9. corn (3rd picture)
10. cow (2nd picture)
11. cereal (1st picture)
12. popcorn (3rd picture)
13. fly in the air (3rd picture)
14. a queen (2nd picture)
15. six legs (3rd picture)
16. ant and bee (1st picture)

Name _____ Date _____

Sample

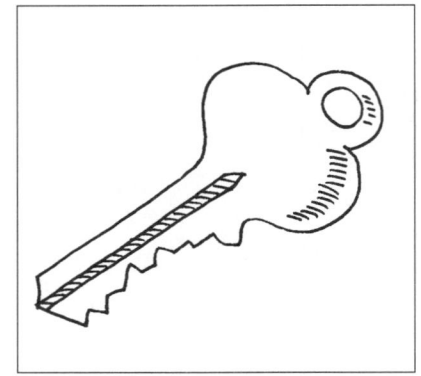

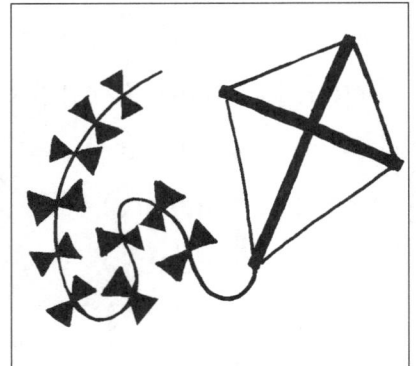

1

2

3

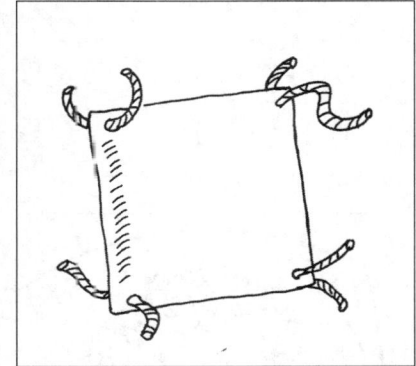

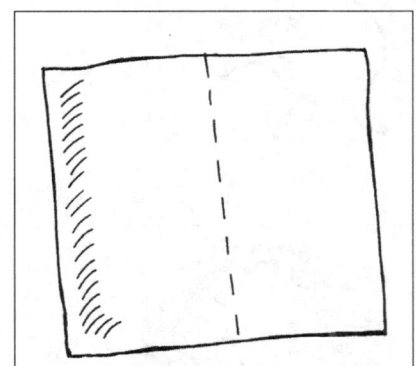

4

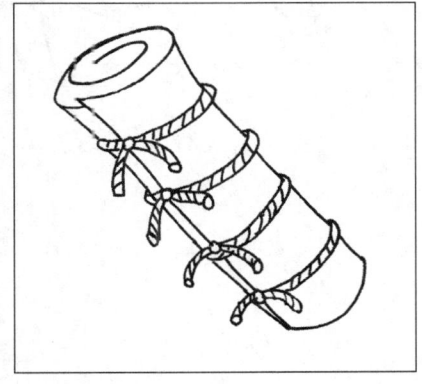

Name _____ Date _____

5

      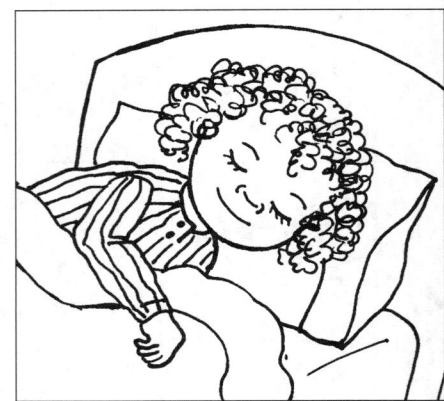

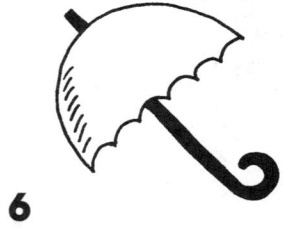

6

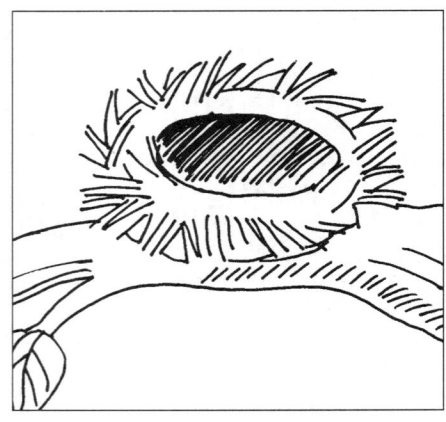      

7

8

Name _____ Date _____

9

10

11

  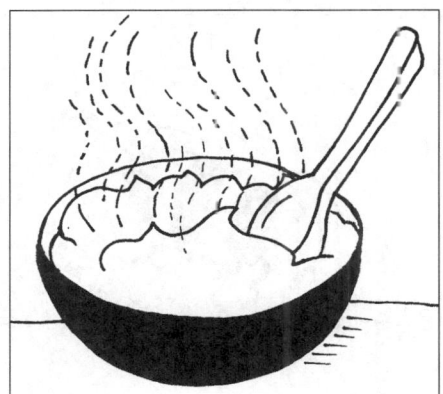

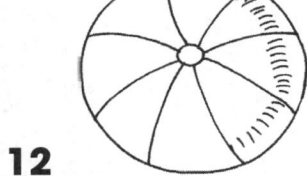

12

Name _____ Date _____

13

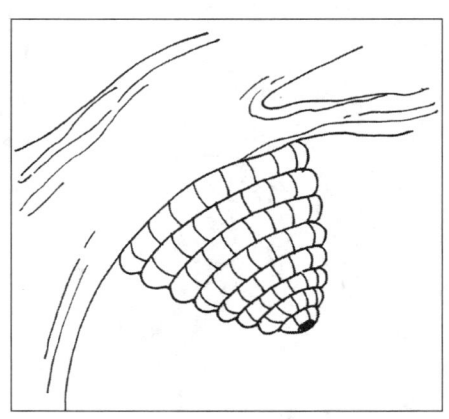

14

  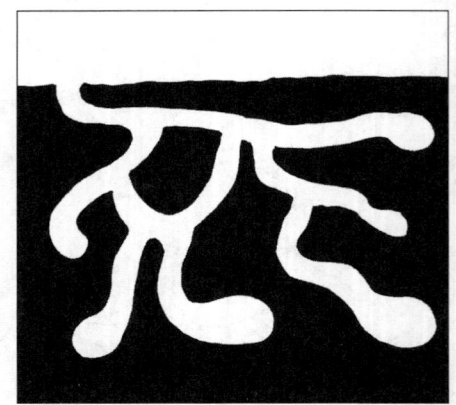

15

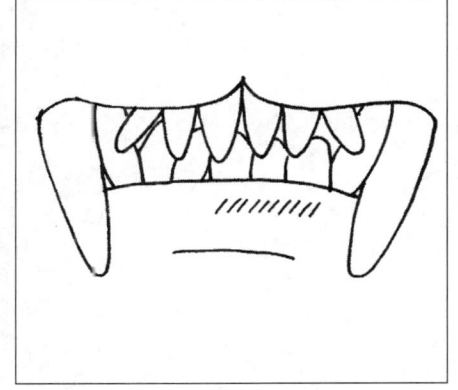 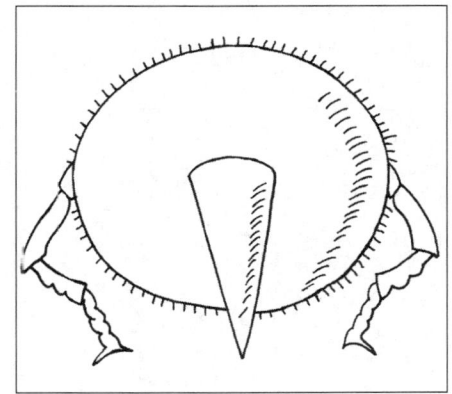 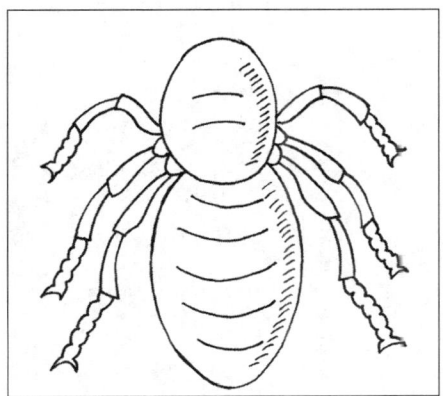

16

Comprehension Strategy Assessment • Grade K

Ongoing Assessments

Assessment 1: Anna's Day
(Analyze Character)
1. sad (3rd picture)
2. splashing in a puddle
   (2nd picture)

Assessment 2: Nick's Garden
(Analyze Character)
1. garden (1st picture)
2. worried (3rd picture)

Assessment 3: Three Eggs
(Analyze Story Elements)
1. in school (1st picture)
2. chicks (2nd picture)

Assessment 4: Mr. Chen
(Analyze Story Elements)
1. suburban scene (2nd picture)
2. raking leaves (3rd picture)

Assessment 5: Wheels
(Compare and Contrast)
1. truck (3rd picture)
2. bicycle (2nd picture)

Assessment 6: Things That Grow
(Compare and Contrast)
1. carrot (3rd picture)
2. pumpkin (1st picture)

Assessment 7: Rosa's Pet
(Draw Conclusions)
1. cat (3rd picture)
2. bowl (1st picture)

Assessment 8: At the Beach
(Draw Conclusions)
1. bathing suits (2nd picture)
2. pails and shovels (1st picture)

Assessment 9: Where Milk Comes From
(Identify Main Idea and Supporting Details)
1. milk (2nd picture)
2. loading onto truck (3rd picture)

Assessment 10: Taking Care of Your Teeth
(Identify Main Idea and Supporting Details)
1. teeth (1st picture)
2. brush your teeth (2nd picture)

Assessment 11: Ethan's Sled
(Identify Cause and Effect)
1. because it was snowing (2nd picture)
2. because he had bare feet (3rd picture)

Assessment 12: The Big Parade
(Identify Cause and Effect)
1. wink (2nd picture)
2. drum (3rd picture)

Assessment 13: Katie the Robin
(Identify Sequence of Events)
1. gather worms (1st picture)
2. makes dandelion tea (2nd picture)

Assessment 14: Having Ice Cream
(Identify Sequence of Events)
1. take out ice cream (1st picture)
2. dog with fudge sauce (3rd picture)

Assessment 15: The Tree House
(Make Inferences)
1. dolls (2nd picture)
2. hammer (1st picture)

Assessment 16: Emily's Crayons
(Make Inferences)
1. to school (2nd picture)
2. toddler (3rd picture)

Assessment 17: A Surprise for Lexy
(Make Predictions)
1. a kitten (3rd picture)
2. excited (2nd picture)

Assessment 18: Pancake Day
(Make Predictions)
1. eat breakfast (2nd picture)
2. pancakes (1st picture)

Assessment 19: Mr. Mendez
(Summarize Information)
1. delivers mail (3rd picture)
2. 2 girls and a boy (3rd picture)

Assessment 20: Tuesdays
(Summarize Information)
1. sitting with the driver (1st picture)
2. grandmother (3rd picture)

This section provides specific directions for administering the Ongoing Comprehension Strategy Assessments to one or more children. When you are ready to begin, give a copy of the pupil page to each child. Make sure each child has a crayon, pencil, or marker for marking their answers. Then proceed by reading the passage and the questions for the assessment. Pause after each question to allow time for children to mark their answers.

For each assessment, read the directions printed in **bold** type.

Ongoing Comprehension Strategy Assessment • 1

Name_____ Date _____

Look at the picture of Anna. Now I am going to read you a story about Anna. Then I will ask you two questions about the story. Listen carefully.

Anna's Day

Rain falls all day long. Anna has to stay inside. She reads some books. She draws some pictures. But Anna is unhappy. She wants to go outside. At last the rain stops. Anna runs outside. She finds a big puddle. Anna jumps right in. She gets wet. She gets muddy. Anna laughs and says, "Now I am having fun!"

---

1. **Put your finger on the row where you see the shoe. Now look at the pictures. How does Anna feel when she is inside the house? Does she feel happy . . . surprised . . . or sad? Draw a circle around the picture that shows how Anna feels when she is inside.**

2. **Move down to the next row where you see the apple. Now look at the pictures. What makes Anna happy? Is it reading a book . . . splashing in a puddle . . . or drawing a picture? Draw a circle around the picture that shows what makes Anna happy.**

Name _____ Date _____

Name_____ Date _____

Look at the picture of Nick. Now I am going to read you a story about Nick. Then I will ask you two questions about the story. Listen carefully.

Nick's Garden

Nick plants some seeds in his garden. Soon flowers grow. The flowers look pretty. They smell sweet. Nick feels proud of his beautiful garden.

Then one day Nick sees a rabbit near his garden. "Uh-oh," says Nick. "That rabbit is hungry. It wants to eat my flowers." But Nick knows what to do. He puts up a fence around his garden. The rabbit cannot get in.

1. **Put your finger on the row where you see the apple. Now look at the pictures. What makes Nick feel proud? Is it his garden . . . the fence . . . or the seeds? Draw a circle around the picture that shows what makes Nick feel proud.**

2. **Move down to the next row where you see the dog. Now look at the pictures. How does Nick feel when he sees the rabbit? Does he feel pleased . . . excited . . . or worried? Draw a circle around the picture that shows how Nick feels when he sees the rabbit.**

Name_____ Date _____

 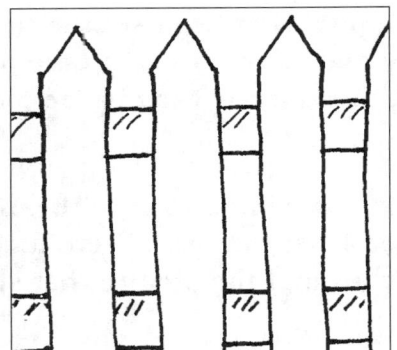 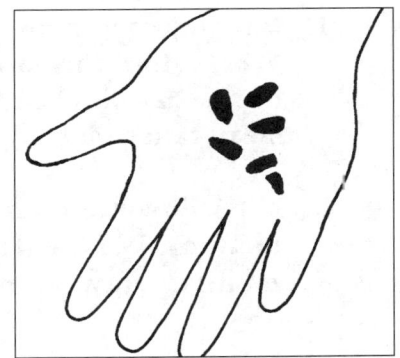

Name_____ Date _____

Look at the picture of the children. Now I am going to read you a story about these children. Then I will ask you two questions about the story. Listen carefully.

Three Eggs

One day Mrs. Trent brought a box to school. "Come and see what's in the box," said Mrs. Trent. The boys and girls looked. They saw three eggs.

"What's inside the eggs?" asked the boys and girls.

Mrs. Trent smiled and said. "Soon the eggs will hatch. Then we will find out."

A few days went by. Then the eggs hatched. Out came three baby chickens.

---

1. **Put your finger on the row where you see the sun. Now look at the pictures. Where does this story take place? Does it take place in school . . . on a farm . . . or in a kitchen? Draw a circle around the picture that shows where the story takes place.**

2. **Move down to the next row where you see the umbrella. Now look at the pictures. What hatched from the eggs? Were they turtles . . . chicks . . . or rabbits? Draw a circle around the picture that shows what hatched from the eggs.**

Name _____ Date _____

  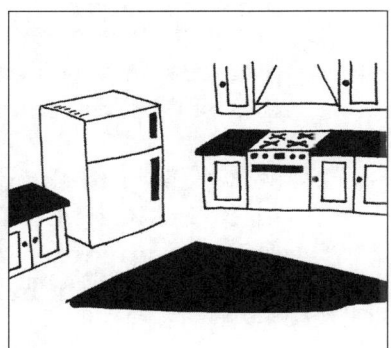

Name_____ Date_____

Look at the picture of Tom and Mr. Chen. Now I am going to read you a story about Tom and Mr. Chen. Then I will ask you two questions about the story. Listen carefully.

Mr. Chen

Mr. Chen and Tom are neighbors. They are friends, too. One day Mr. Chen was raking leaves in his yard. Tom said, "I'll help you, Mr. Chen."

So Tom and Mr. Chen raked the leaves together. When they were done, Mr. Chen said, "Now I want to thank you for your help, Tom." Mr. Chen went into his house. He came back with a plate of cookies. "These are for you, Tom," he said.

---

1. **Put your finger on the row where you see the teddy bear. Now look at the pictures. Where does this story take place? Draw a circle around the picture that shows where the story takes place.**

2. **Move down to the next row where you see the house. Now look at the pictures. How did Tom help Mr. Chen? Did he help by mopping the floor . . . painting a fence . . . or raking leaves? Draw a circle around the picture that shows how Tom helped Mr. Chen.**

Name_____ Date_____

Name_____ Date_____

Look at the picture. Now I am going to read you a story. Then I will ask you two questions about the story. Listen carefully.

Wheels

Wheels help us go. Some wheels are small. The skateboard has little wheels. The wagon does, too. But some wheels are very big. See how big the truck's wheels are! How many wheels do you need to go from here to there? The car and the wagon have four wheels. But you can get around on two wheels. Just hop on your bike and go!

---

1. **Put your finger on the row where you see the fish. Now look at the pictures. Which one has the biggest wheels? Is it the wagon . . . the skateboard . . . or the truck? Draw a circle around the one that has the biggest wheels.**

2. **Move down to the next row where you see the cat. Now look at the pictures. Which one has fewer wheels than the others? Is it the car . . . the bicycle . . . or the wagon? Draw a circle around the one that has fewer wheels.**

Name _____ Date _____

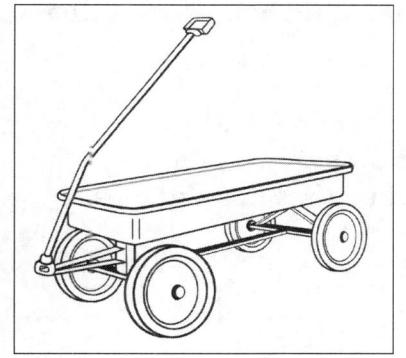  

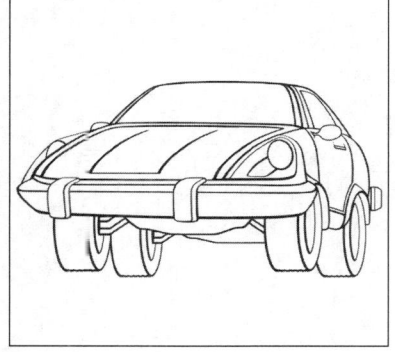  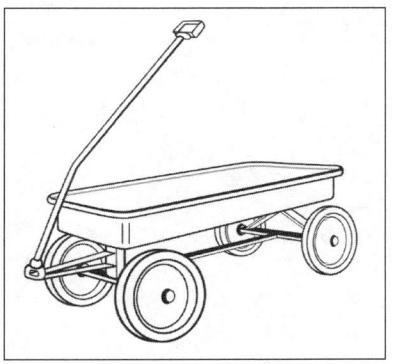

Name_____ Date _____

Look at the picture. Now I am going to read you a story. Then I will ask you two questions about the story. Listen carefully.

Things That Grow

Pumpkins grow on vines. Peaches grow on trees. Carrots grow under the ground. You can pick pumpkins or peaches. But you must pull carrots out of the ground. Inside a pumpkin there are many small seeds. A peach has only one big seed. But what about a carrot? A carrot does not have any seeds inside.

---

1. **Put your finger on the row where you see the moon. Now look at the pictures. Which one grows under the ground? Is it the peach . . . the pumpkin . . . or the carrot? Draw a circle around the one that grows under the ground.**

2. **Move down to the next row where you see the ball. Now look at the pictures. Which one has the most seeds? Is it the pumpkin . . . the carrot . . . or the peach? Draw a circle around the one that has the most seeds.**

Name ———————————————————————— Date ————————

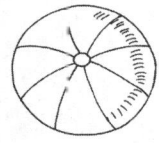

Name_____ Date_____

Look at the picture. Now I am going to read you a story. Then I will ask you two questions about the story. Listen carefully.

Rosa's Pet

Rosa stared out the window. "I wish Dusty would come home," she said.

"Don't worry," Dad replied. "Dusty will come back when he's hungry."

Just then there was a loud meow at the door. Rosa opened the door wide. Dusty dashed inside and hurried to his food dish.

1. **Put your finger on the row where you see the sock. Now look at the pictures. What kind of pet is Dusty? Is Dusty a bird . . . a dog . . . or a cat? Draw a circle around the picture that shows what kind of pet Dusty is.**

2. **Move down to the next row where you see the paintbrush. Now look at the pictures. What does Dusty eat? Does Dusty eat food from a bowl . . . does he eat a sandwich . . . or does he eat bird seed? Draw a circle around the picture that shows what Dusty eats.**

Name _____ Date _____

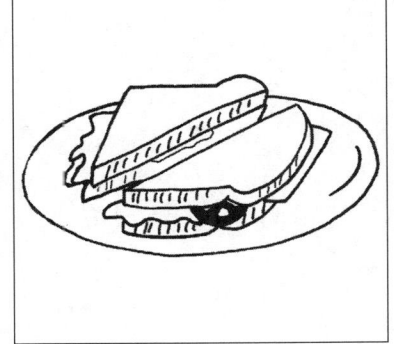

Name_____ Date_____

Look at the picture. Now I am going to read you a story. Then I will ask you two questions about the story. Listen carefully.

At the Beach

Mama took Ruby and Carl to the beach. Carl wanted to swim. But Ruby wanted to make a sand castle. "What can I use to make my castle?" asked Ruby. Mama handed Ruby a bag. Ruby looked inside and said, "Thanks, Mama. This is just what I need!"

---

1. Put your finger on the row where you see the book. Now look at the pictures. Which picture shows how Ruby and Carl looked in this story? Draw a circle around the picture that shows how Ruby and Carl looked.

2. Move down to the next row where you see the truck. Now look at the pictures. What did Ruby see in the bag? Draw a circle around the picture that shows what Ruby saw in the bag.

Name _____ Date _____

  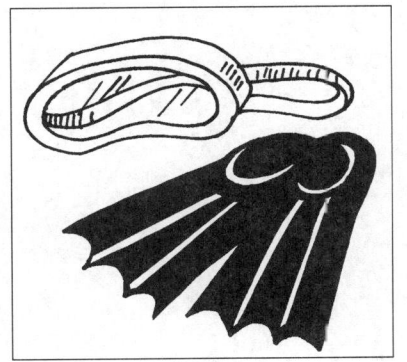

Name_____ Date_____

Look at the picture. Now I am going to read you a story. Then I will ask you two questions about the story. Listen carefully.

Where Milk Comes From

You buy milk at the store. But how did it get there? Milk comes from cows that live at a dairy farm. Farmers milk the cows. They send the milk to a factory. Workers at the factory make sure the milk is safe to drink. Then they put the milk into containers. The containers go on a truck. The truck brings the containers to the store. Now the milk is ready for you to buy.

---

1. Put your finger on the row where you see the shoe. Now look at the pictures. Which picture shows what this story is mostly about? Draw a circle around the picture that shows what this story is mostly about.

2. Move down to the next row where you see the apple. Now look at the pictures. What happens at the factory? Draw a circle around the picture that shows what happens at the factory.

Name _____ Date _____

Name_____ Date _____

Look at the picture. Now I am going to read you a story. Then I will ask you two questions about the story. Listen carefully.

Taking Care of Your Teeth

Your teeth are important. How can you take care of them? Here are three rules to follow. First, brush your teeth twice a day. Brush after breakfast and before you go to bed. Second, stay away from too many sweets. Candy and soda pop can make your teeth weak. Third, visit your dentist at least once a year. Your dentist will check your teeth and get them super clean!

---

1. **Put your finger on the row where you see the star. Now look at the pictures. Which picture shows what this story is mostly about? Draw a circle around the picture that shows what this story is mostly about.**

2. **Move down to the next row where you see the dog. Now look at the pictures. What should you do twice a day? Should you drink soda pop . . . brush your teeth . . . or visit the dentist? Draw a circle around the picture of something you should do twice a day.**

Name _____ Date _____

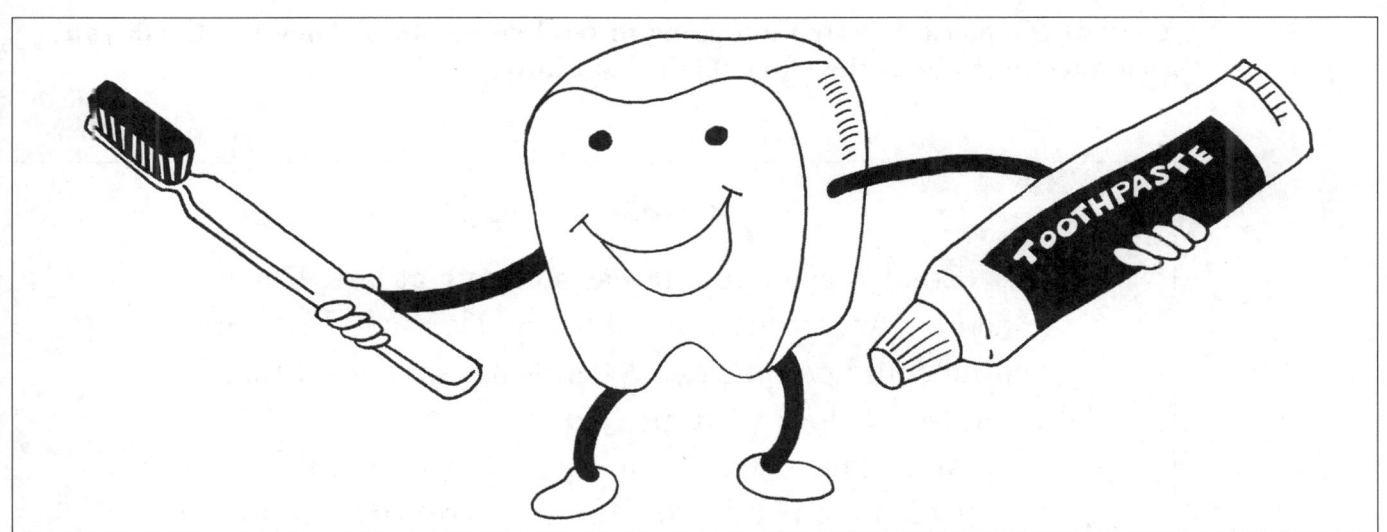

  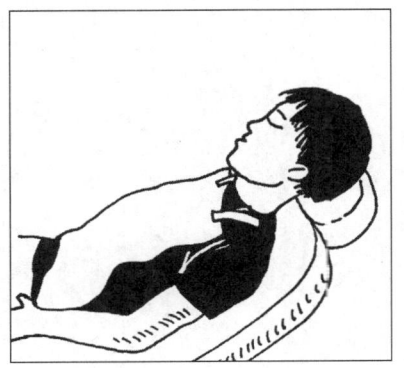

Name_____ Date_____

Look at the picture. Now I am going to read you a story. Then I will ask you two questions about the story. Listen carefully.

Ethan's Sled

Ethan was happy. It was snowing at last! Ethan had a new sled he wanted to try. He asked his mom if he could go outside. When Mom said yes, Ethan ran to the door with his sled.

Mom said, "Aren't you forgetting something?"

Ethan looked down. His feet were bare! He found his boots and pulled them on. Soon he was flying down the hill on his new sled. He was glad his boots kept his toes warm!

---

1. Put your finger on the row where you see the sun. Now look at the pictures. Why was Ethan happy? Was it because it was his birthday . . . because it was snowing . . . or because he had a new dog? Draw a circle around the picture that shows why Ethan was happy.

2. Move down to the next row where you see the umbrella. Now look at the pictures. Why did Mom ask if Ethan was forgetting something? Was it because he was in his pajamas . . . because he was wearing a party hat . . . or because he had bare feet? Draw a circle around the picture that shows why Mom asked if Ethan was forgetting something.

Name _____ Date _____

Name_____ Date_____

Look at the picture. Now I am going to read you a story. Then I will ask you two questions about the story. Listen carefully.

The Big Parade

Today is the day of the big parade. Michael and his big brother Jason stand on the sidewalk. They wait and wait. Lots of people are waiting. Then Michael hears some music. "They're coming!" he shouts. Sure enough, a marching band comes around the corner. The drum goes "Boom! Boom! Boom!" Then come the clowns. They wear silly clothes. All of a sudden, one of the clowns comes right over to Michael. At first, he is scared. Then the clown winks at him. Now Michael knows the clown is really his grandpa! Michael winks back. He is proud to know that his grandpa is in the parade!

1. Put your finger on the row where you see the teddy bear. Now look at the pictures. How did Michael know that the clown was really his grandpa? Did the clown frown . . . wink . . . or take off his hat? Draw a circle around the picture that shows how Michael knew.

2. Put your finger on the row where you see the house. Now look at the pictures. What made a loud noise in the story? Was it a fire engine . . . a thunderstorm . . . or a drum? Draw a circle around the picture that shows what made a loud noise.

Name _____ Date _____

  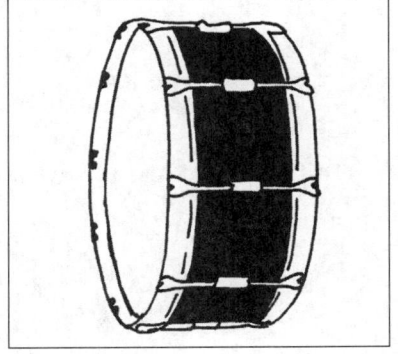

Name_____ Date_____

Now I am going to read you a story. Then I will ask you two questions about the story. Listen carefully.

Katie the Robin

Katie the robin lives in a big tree. Most of Katie's friends live nearby. One day, Katie decides to have a party for her friends. First, she gathers lots of worms and seeds for them to eat. Then she picks some flowers—red ones, yellow ones, and pink ones. Finally, she makes some dandelion tea. Now she is ready. The party can begin.

---

1. Put your finger on the row where you see the fish. Now look at the pictures. What does Katie the robin do first? Does she gather worms . . . pick flowers . . . or wrap presents? Draw a circle around the picture that shows what Katie does first.

2. Move down to the next row where you see the cat. Now look at the pictures. What does Katie do last? Does she pick flowers . . . make dandelion tea . . . or take a nap? Draw a circle around the picture that shows what Katie does last.

Name _____ Date _____

Name_____ Date _____

Look at the picture. Now I am going to read you a story. Then I will ask you two questions about the story. Listen carefully.

Having Ice Cream

Keisha and Hannah love ice cream. One day they decided to make ice cream treats. First, Keisha took the ice cream out of the freezer. Then Hannah got out the fudge sauce. Next, the two girls together put the ice cream into bowls. Then Hannah started to pour fudge sauce onto the ice cream. Oops! The fudge sauce spilled all over the floor. Their dog, Prince, came over and sniffed the fudge sauce. When he looked up, he had a chocolate mustache! Keisha and Hannah laughed and laughed.

1. **Put your finger on the row where you see the moon. Now look at the pictures. What did the girls do first in this story? Did they take out the ice cream . . . get out the fudge sauce . . . or put ice cream into bowls? Draw a circle around the picture that shows what the girls did first.**

2. **Move down to the next row where you see the ball. Now look at the pictures. What happened last in the story? Draw a circle around the picture that shows what happened last.**

Name _____ Date _____

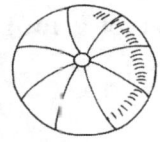

Name_____ Date _____

Look at the picture. Now I am going to read you a story. Then I will ask you two questions about the story. Listen carefully.

The Tree House

Maria wanted a tree house. Her dad said he would build one. Dad asked, "What will you do in your tree house?"

Maria said, "I want to play house with Cathy and Patty."

Dad got a saw and some boards. He cut the boards. Then he nailed them onto the tree. Soon the tree house was finished. Maria and her dad put the things she wanted inside. Then Maria moved into her new tree house and played there for hours.

1. Put your finger on the row where you see the sock. Now look at the pictures. Which things did Maria and her dad put in the tree house for her to play with? Were they coloring books . . . dolls . . . or toy blocks? Draw a circle around the picture that shows what Maria and her dad put in the tree house.

2. Move down to the next row where you see the paintbrush. Now look at the pictures. Which tool did Dad use to build the tree house? Did he use a hammer . . . a rake . . . or a drill? Draw a circle around the picture of a tool that Dad used.

Name _____ Date _____

Name_____ Date_____

Look at the picture. Now I am going to read you a story. Then I will ask you two questions about the story. Listen carefully.

Emily's Crayons

Emily got a new box of crayons. One morning she put them on the table. Then she ran out the front door to get the bus. When she came home that afternoon, she wanted to color. Emily went to the table to get her crayons. She opened the box. Someone had taken off all the wrappers! Emily looked under the table. There was her brother Nate, throwing crayon wrappers in the air. "Mom!" shouted Emily, "Look at what Nate did!" Mom came in and looked under the table. Just then Nate piled all the wrappers on his head. Mom started to laugh. Pretty soon Emily was laughing, too.

---

1. **Put your finger on the row where you see the book. Now look at the pictures. Where did Emily go during the day? Did she go to work . . . to school . . . or to the movies? Draw a circle around the picture that shows where Emily went during the day.**

2. **Move down to the next row where you see the truck. Now look at the pictures. Which picture shows what Nate looks like? Draw a circle around the picture of Nate.**

Name _____ Date _____

  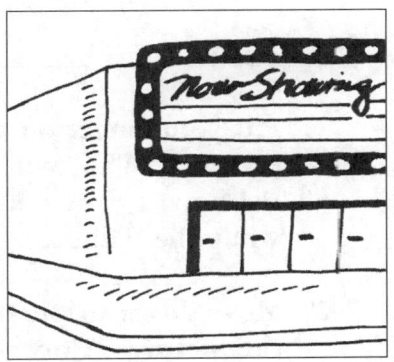

Name_____ Date_____

Look at the picture. Now I am going to read you a story. Then I will ask you two questions about the story. Listen carefully.

A Surprise for Lexy

Lexy's birthday was coming soon. All she wanted for her birthday was a kitten. Her dad said, "Oh, I don't know about that, Lexy. We'll see."

Two days later, it was Lexy's birthday. At breakfast she got a new bracelet and a book and a box of paints—but no kitten! She was so sad.

That afternoon, her dad picked her up from school. Lexy got in the back seat. There was a cardboard box on the seat. Dad said, "I have a surprise for you. Take a look in that box." All of a sudden, the box moved!

---

1. Put your finger on the row where you see the shoe. Now look at the pictures. What will Lexy see in the box? Will it be a bracelet . . . a fishbowl . . . or a kitten? Draw a circle around the picture that shows what she will see.

2. Move down to the next row where you see the apple. Now look at the pictures. How will Lexy feel about the surprise? Will she feel afraid . . . excited . . . or sad? Draw a circle around the picture that shows how Lexy will feel.

Name _____ Date _____

Name_____ Date_____

Look at the picture. Now I am going to read you a story. Then I will ask you two questions about the story. Listen carefully.

Pancake Day

Every year on June 5th, the Wilson family has Pancake Day. Mom and Dad get up early and make pancakes for breakfast. But this year, before they can start eating, Jermaine asks, "Why do we have Pancake Day?"

Mom laughs and says, "Because I met your dad at a pancake breakfast, and he spilled peaches all over me." Dad makes a silly face and says, "We have a special breakfast every year because your mom likes to remind me. Just be glad it wasn't broccoli."

---

1. **Put your finger on the row where you see the star. Now look at the pictures. What will Mr. Wilson do next? Will he have a birthday cake . . . eat breakfast . . . or buy some peaches? Draw a circle around the picture that shows what will happen next.**

2. **Move down to the next row where you see the dog. Now look at the pictures. What will the Wilsons have for breakfast? Will they have pancakes . . . broccoli . . . or peaches? Draw a circle around the picture that shows what the Wilsons will have for breakfast.**

Name _____ Date _____

Name_____ Date_____

Look at the picture. Now I am going to read you a story. Then I will ask you two questions about the story. Listen carefully.

Mr. Mendez

Mr. Mendez is a letter carrier. Most people call him the mailman. Every morning he takes his children Paula, Lita, and Dan, to school. Then he goes to the post office. He gets all the mail for his route and puts it in his cart. Then he walks up and down the streets of our neighborhood. He delivers the mail to every house. People like Mr. Mendez. He is always nice to everyone.

---

1. **Put your finger on the row where you see the sun. Now look at the pictures. What does Mr. Mendez do in his job? Draw a circle around the picture that shows what Mr. Mendez does.**

2. **Move down to the next row where you see the umbrella. Now look at the pictures. Which picture shows Mr. Mendez's children? Draw a circle around the picture that shows the Mendez children.**

Name _____ Date _____

Name_____ Date _____

Look at the picture. Now I am going to read you a story. Then I will ask you two questions about the story. Listen carefully.

Tuesdays

Yoshi loves Tuesdays. That's the day his grandmother takes him to the train station with her. Yoshi gets to see trains coming and going. They are very big and noisy, but Yoshi isn't scared. He likes to pretend that he is riding on a train.

One day, Yoshi's grandmother says, "Would you like to see where the train driver sits?" Right away Yoshi says yes. Soon he and his grandmother are sitting in the front of the train with the driver. Yoshi even gets to blow the train's horn! This is the best Tuesday ever!

1. **Put your finger on the row where you see the teddy bear. Now look at the pictures. Which picture shows what happens on the best Tuesday ever? Draw a circle around the picture that shows what happens on that day.**

2. **Move down to the next row where you see the house. Now look at the pictures. Who takes Yoshi to the train station on Tuesdays? Is it his father . . . his mother . . . or his grandmother? Draw a circle around the picture that shows who takes Yoshi to the train station.**

Name _____ Date _____

DIRECTIONS FOR ADMINISTERING THE MIDYEAR TEST

Today I am going to read some stories. I will ask you some questions about each story. Listen carefully and follow along as I read. Then answer each question. First I will read a practice question.

Sample

> I am going to read a sentence about a girl named Sheri. Then I am going to ask a question. Listen to this sentence:
>
> Sheri wants to eat a sandwich.
>
> Now put your finger on the row where you see the little toy car. Now look at the pictures. What does Sheri want to eat? Does she want to eat cereal . . . a sandwich . . . or a banana? Draw a circle around the picture that shows what Sheri wants to eat. (Pause.) You should have made a circle around the picture of the sandwich. That is the correct answer.

Answer any questions that children may have. When children are ready, administer the test by reading these directions. Check to make sure children are on the correct page.

Now I am going to read you a story about Peppy the Pig. Then I will ask two questions about the story. Listen carefully.

> Peppy the Pig woke up one morning. He was very hungry. He went to the trough where the farmer usually put his food. The trough was empty! "Where is my breakfast?" asked Peppy. "I don't know!" said Herbert the Horse. "The farmer never sleeps this late." Just then, the farmer opened the door and came into the place where the animals lived. The farmer gave the horse some hay. Then he filled Peppy's trough with food. "Hurray!" said Peppy.

1. **Put your finger on the row where you see the shoe. Now look at the pictures. In this story, where is Peppy? Is he in a field . . . in a mud puddle . . . or in a barn? Draw a circle around the picture that shows where Peppy is.**

2. **Move down to the next row where you see the apple. Now look at the pictures. How does Peppy feel when the farmer brings some food? Does he feel happy . . . surprised . . . or angry? Draw a circle around the picture that shows how Peppy feels when the farmer brings some food.**

Tell children to turn to the next page.

Now I am going to read a story about something you can make. Then I will ask two questions about the story. Listen carefully.

You can make a simple, little puppet out of a wooden craft stick. First, use a black marker to draw two eyes near the top of the stick. Then cut a dress out of paper and glue it to the stick. Last, glue a cotton ball to the top of the stick. The cotton ball will be your puppet's hair. You can hold the puppet by the bottom of the stick and move it around.

3. **Put your finger on the first row where you see the star. Now look at the pictures. What should you do first? Should you glue the cotton ball to the stick . . . cut a dress out of paper . . . or draw eyes on the stick? Draw a circle around the picture that shows what you should do first.**

4. **Move down to the next row where you see the dog. Now look at the pictures. If you follow these directions, what do you have when you finish? Draw a circle around the picture that shows what you have when you finish.**

Tell children to turn to the next page.

Now I am going to read you a story about a boy named Nate. Then I will ask four questions about the story. Listen carefully.

Nate came into the kitchen one Saturday morning. His dad was trying to make pancakes, but he was having trouble. "I have lost my glasses," said Dad. "I can't read the recipe book!" Nate looked next to the sink. The glasses were not there. Nate looked on the shelf. The glasses were not there either. Nate thought hard. Then he remembered where he had seen his father's glasses! He looked on his father's desk. The glasses were sitting next to the computer!

5. **Put your finger on the row where you see the sun. Now look at the pictures. In this story, what will happen next? Will Nate put on the glasses . . . give the glasses to his father . . . or put the glasses away? Draw a circle around the picture that shows what Nate will do next.**

6. **Move down to the next row where you see the umbrella. Now look at the pictures. Where did Nate find the glasses? Did he find them next to the sink . . . on a shelf . . . or next to the computer? Draw a circle around the picture that shows where Nate found the glasses.**

Tell children to turn to the next page.

7. **Put your finger on the row where you see the teddy bear. Now look at the pictures. What does Nate do at the beginning of the story? Does he come into the kitchen . . . find some glasses . . . or eat some pancakes? Draw a circle around the picture that shows what Nate does at the beginning of the story.**

8. **Move down to the next row where you see the house. Now look at the pictures. How does Dad feel when he tries to read the recipe book? Does he feel upset . . . sleepy . . . or happy? Draw a circle around the picture that shows how Dad feels when he tries to read the recipe book.**

Tell children to turn to the next page.

Now I am going to read a story about an animal. Then I will ask four questions about the story. Listen carefully.

Beavers are furry animals with big, sharp teeth. They eat bark, twigs, and other parts of trees. Beavers are good swimmers. Sometimes they live in holes in riverbanks. But most beavers make houses called lodges in ponds. To make these lodges, beavers first chew on trees. They chew until the trees fall down! The beavers drag the pieces of wood into the pond. They pile it up into a round shape. They build a living space inside. They cover the lodge with mud. Then they have a safe place to live.

---

9. **Put your finger on the row where you see the fish. Now look at the pictures. What is this story mostly about? Is it about beavers . . . trees . . . or houses? Draw a circle around the picture that shows what the story is mostly about.**

10. **Move down to the next row where you see the cat. Now look at the pictures. Where do most beavers build their lodges? Do they build them in a riverbank . . . in a pond . . . or in a tree? Draw a circle around the picture that shows where most beavers build their lodges.**

Tell children to turn to the next page.

11. **Put your finger on the row where you see the moon. Now look at the pictures. How do beavers cut down trees? Do they use their tails . . . their claws . . . or their teeth? Draw a circle around the picture of what beavers use to cut down trees.**

12. **Move down to the next row where you see the ball. Now look at the pictures. Which picture shows something that a beaver would most likely eat? Would a beaver probably eat a frog . . . a bee . . . or a leaf? Draw a circle around the picture of the thing that a beaver would most likely eat.**

Tell children to turn to the next page.

Now I am going to read a story about oak trees and pine trees. Then I will ask four questions about the story. Listen carefully.

Oak trees and pine trees both grow in America. Oaks and pines are alike in some ways. Both have trunks and branches. Like all trees, they need sunlight and rain to grow. They produce wood used to make houses and furniture. But oaks and pines are different in some ways, too. Oak trees have leaves on their branches. Pine trees have needles instead of leaves. Most oak trees are bare in winter because their leaves fall off in autumn. Pine trees are green all year round. Oak trees drop nuts called acorns. Pine trees drop cones instead of acorns.

13.   Put your finger on the row where you see the sock. Now look at the pictures. How are oak trees different from pine trees? Is it because oak trees need rain to grow . . . have branches . . . or become bare in winter? Draw a circle around the way oak trees are different from pine trees.

14.   Move down to the next row where you see the paintbrush. Now look at the pictures. Oak trees and pine trees both have what? Do they both have trunks . . . leaves . . . or needles? Draw a circle around the thing both oak trees and pine trees have.

Tell children to turn to the next page.

15. Put your finger on the row where you see the book. Now look at the pictures. You can tell from the story that all trees produce what? Acorns . . . wood . . . or cones? Draw a circle around the thing all trees produce.

16. Move down to the next row where you see the truck. Now look at the pictures. Which picture shows what you learned about in this story? Draw a circle around the picture that shows what you learned about in this story.

1. in a barn (3rd picture)
2. happy (1st picture)
3. draw eyes on the stick (3rd picture)
4. stick puppet (2nd picture)
5. gives glasses to father (2nd picture)
6. next to the computer (3rd picture)
7. comes into the kitchen (1st picture)
8. upset (1st picture)
9. beavers (1st picture)
10. in a pond (2nd picture)
11. teeth (3rd picture)
12. leaf (3rd picture)
13. bare in winter (3rd picture)
14. trunks (1st picture)
15. wood (2nd picture)
16. oak and pine trees (2nd picture)

Name _____ Date _____

Sample

1

2

3

 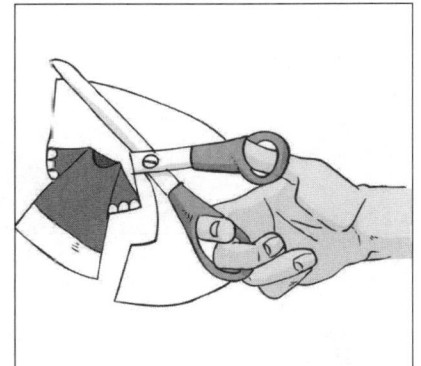 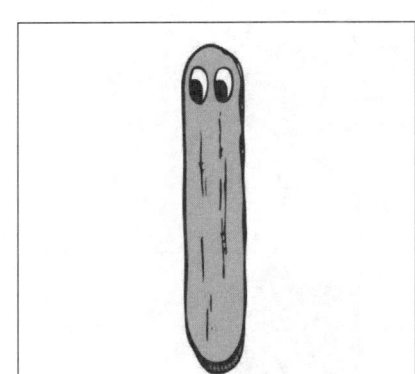

4

Comprehension Strategy Assessment • Grade K

Name _____ Date _____

5

6

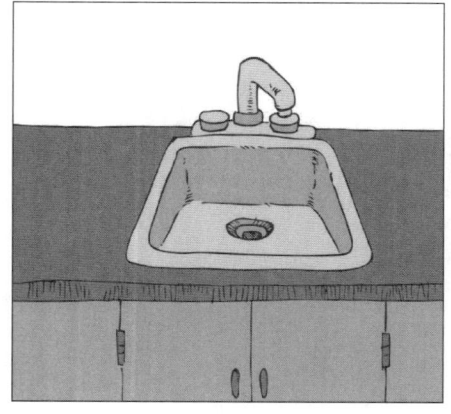

7

8

Name _____ Date _____

9

10

  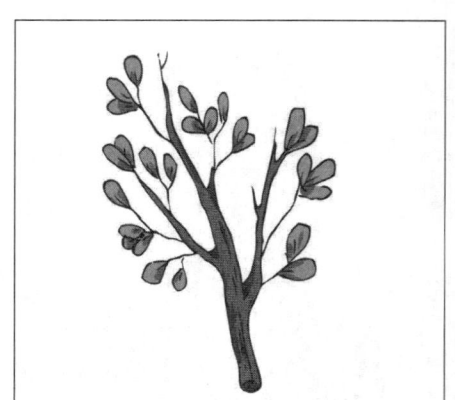

11

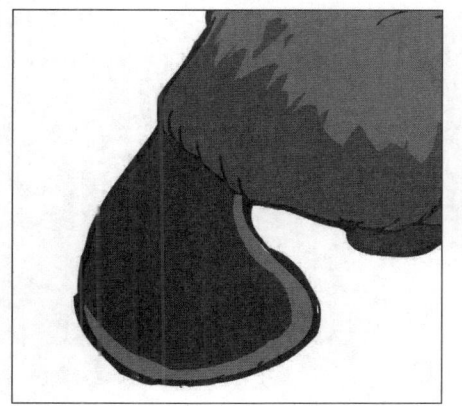 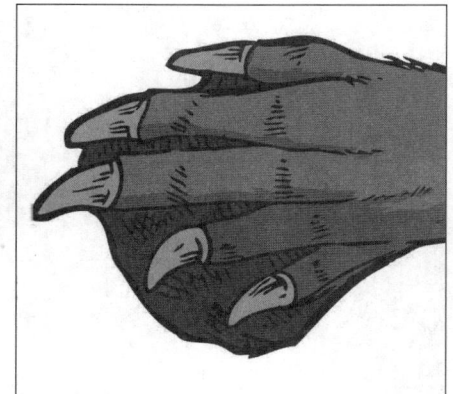 

12

Name _____ Date _____

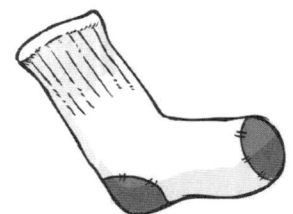

13

14

15

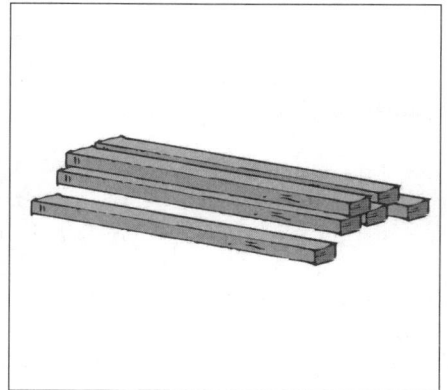

16

DIRECTIONS FOR ADMINISTERING THE POSTTEST

This section provides specific directions for administering the Posttest to one or more children. When you are ready to begin, read through the sample question and instruct children to mark their answers. Hold up a copy of the test page with the answer circled as a model to show what it looks like. Then proceed with the Posttest by reading the passages and items. Pause after each question to allow time for children to mark their answers.

To begin, be sure children have the first page of the Posttest in front of them. Read the directions printed in **bold** type.

Today I am going to read some stories. I will ask you some questions about each story. Listen carefully and follow along as I read. Then answer each question. First we will read a practice question.

Sample

> I am going to read a sentence about a girl named Emma. Then I am going to ask a question. Listen to this sentence:
>
> Emma has a new kite with a long tail.
>
> Now put your finger on the row where you see the little toy car. Now look at the pictures. What does Emma have? Does she have a flower . . . a key . . . or a kite? Draw a circle around the picture that shows what Emma has. (Pause.) You should have made a circle around the kite. That is the correct answer.

Answer any questions that children may have. When children are ready, administer the test by reading these directions. Check to make sure children are on the correct page.

Now I am going to read you a story about Sandy Squirrel. Then I will ask you two questions about the story. Listen carefully.

> Sandy Squirrel looks across the deep, blue water. She says, "I see a patch of ripe berries on the other side. But how can I get there? I can't swim."
> Just then, Tommy Turtle pokes his head out of the water. "Hop on my back," says Tommy. "I'll take you to the other side."
> Sandy says, "Oh, thank you, Tommy!" Then she hops on the turtle's back.

1. **Put your finger on the row where you see the shoe. Now look at the pictures. In this story, where is Sandy Squirrel? Is she on a boat . . . near a pond . . . or by a pool? Draw a circle around the picture that shows where Sandy is.**

2. **Move down to the next row where you see the apple. Now look at the pictures. How does Sandy feel about riding on Tommy's back? Does she feel scared . . . angry . . . or happy? Draw a circle around the picture that shows how Sandy feels about riding on Tommy's back.**

Tell children to turn to the next page.

Now I am going to read a story about something you can make.

Here's an easy way to make a make a sunny face mask. You need a paper plate, scissors, glue, and some gold glitter. First, have a grown-up cut out two eye holes. Then squeeze out lines of glue all around the edge of the plate. Add a curved line of glue for a big smile. Sprinkle on the glitter to cover all the glue. When the glue is dry, you'll be ready to shine.

3. **Put your finger on the first row where you see the star. Now look at the pictures. What should you do first? Should you put glue on the plate . . . have a grown-up cut the eye holes . . . or sprinkle on the glitter? Draw a circle around the picture that shows what you should do first.**

4. **Move down to the next row where you see the dog. Now look at the pictures. If you follow these directions, what do you have when you finish? Draw a circle around the picture that shows what you have when you finish.**

Tell children to turn to the next page.

Now I am going to read a story about a boy named James. Then I will ask four questions about the story. Listen carefully.

On Wednesday, James came home from school at 3 o'clock. When he walked into his apartment, he found a note on the table. The note said, "James, please hang up your coat. Then put your lunchbox away. After that, you can have a snack. You will find a glass of milk in the refrigerator and a granola bar on the table. I will be home in a few minutes. Love, Mom." Just then, the kitty door opened and Stripes came in. "Hi, Stripes," said James. "You're just in time to have a snack with me."

5. **Put your finger on the row where you see the sun. Now look at the pictures. In this story, what will happen next? Will James make a sandwich for lunch . . . put his lunchbox away . . . or hang up his coat? Draw a circle around the picture that shows what will happen next.**

6. **Move down to the next row where you see the umbrella. Now look at the pictures. Where does this story take place? Does it take place in school . . . at James's home . . . or at the store? Draw a circle around the picture that shows where the story takes place.**

Tell children to turn to the next page.

7. **Put your finger on the row where you see the teddy bear. Now look at the pictures. What happens at the end of the story? Does James come home from school . . . does James have a snack . . . or does Stripes come in through the kitty door? Draw a circle around the picture that shows what happens at the end of the story.**

8. **Move down to the next row where you see the house. Now look at the pictures. How does James feel when he sees Stripes? Does he feel happy . . . surprised . . . or sad? Draw a circle around the picture that shows how James feels when he sees Stripes.**

Tell children to turn to the next page.

Now I am going to read a story about a kind of animal. Then I will ask four questions about the story. Listen carefully.

> Gerbils are funny little animals. They look a lot like mice. Most gerbils are brown, black, or white. Gerbils usually live in the desert, so they like hot weather and sun. Gerbils make good pets because they are friendly and easy to take care of. They like to eat seeds, nuts, and some greens. Sometimes they will eat vegetables, such as carrots. They need water every day and plenty of exercise. They also need things to chew on, such as cardboard. This keeps their teeth from growing too much.

9. **Put your finger on the row where you see the fish. Now look at the pictures. What is this story mostly about? Is it about the desert . . . gerbils . . . or vegetables? Draw a circle around the picture that shows what the story is mostly about.**

10. **Move down to the next row where you see the cat. Now look at the pictures. Which animal looks most like a gerbil? Is it a bird . . . a dog . . . or a mouse? Draw a circle around the picture of the animal that looks most like a gerbil.**

Tell children to turn to the next page.

11. **Put your finger on the row where you see the moon. Now look at the pictures. Why do gerbils like hot weather and sun? Is it because they come from the desert . . . because they need plenty of exercise . . . or because they like to eat seeds and nuts? Draw a circle around the picture that shows why gerbils like hot weather and sun.**

12. **Move down to the next row where you see the ball. Now look at the pictures. Which food would gerbils probably like? Would they like a tuna fish sandwich . . . sunflower seeds . . . or a banana? Draw a circle around the picture that shows food that gerbils would probably like.**

Tell children to turn to the next page.

Now I am going to read a story about lizards and frogs. Then I will ask four questions about the story. Listen carefully.

> Lizards and frogs live in many places. Most lizards like hot, dry areas. They love to lie in the sun. Some lizards can run very quickly, and some are good climbers. Most frogs live in or near water. They like cool, wet places. Unlike lizards, frogs are good swimmers and they like to jump. But they can't run or climb. Frogs can breathe in the water and in air. Lizards and frogs seem very different, but they are alike in some ways. Both lizards and frogs eat bugs and flies. Both have four legs, and both lay eggs.

13. **Put your finger on the row where you see the sock. Now look at the pictures. What can many lizards do that frogs cannot do? Can lizards swim . . . breathe in the water . . . or climb? Draw a circle around the picture of something that many lizards can do but frogs cannot.**

14. **Move down to the next row where you see the paintbrush. Now look at the pictures. How are frogs and lizards alike? Do they both like hot dry, places . . . eat bugs and flies . . . or live in water? Draw a circle around the picture of one way frogs and lizards are alike.**

Tell children to turn to the next page.

15. **Put your finger on the row where you see the book. Now look at the pictures. In which of these places would you find the most lizards? Draw a circle around the picture of the place where you would find the most lizards.**

16. **Move down to the next row where you see the truck. Now look at the pictures. Which picture shows something you learned about in this story? Draw a circle around the picture that shows something you learned about in the story.**

1. near a pond (2nd picture)

2. happy (3rd picture)

3. cut the eye holes
   (2nd picture)

4. plate with face
   (3rd picture)

5. hang up his coat
   (3rd picture)

6. at James's home
   (2nd picture)

7. Stripes comes in
   (3rd picture)

8. happy (1st picture)

9. gerbils (2nd picture)

10. mouse (3rd picture)

11. because they come from desert
    (1st picture)

12. sunflower seeds
    (2nd picture)

13. climb (3rd picture)

14. Both eat bugs and flies. (2nd picture)

15. desert (2nd picture)

16. lizard and frog (1st picture)

Posttest Answer Key

Name _____ Date _____

Sample

 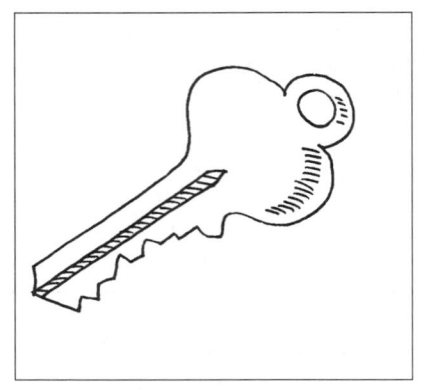 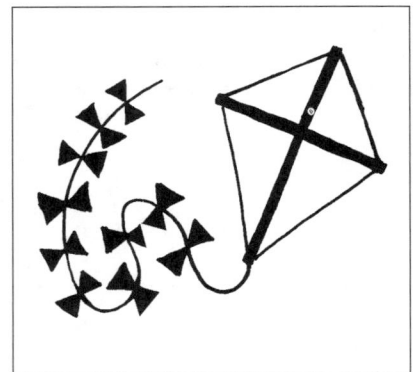

1

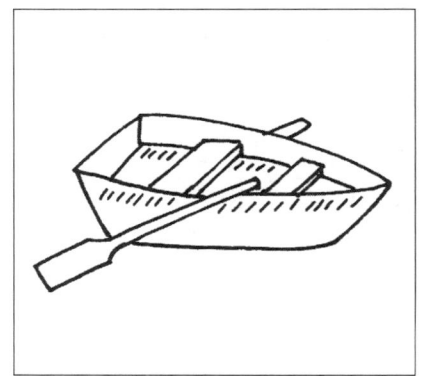  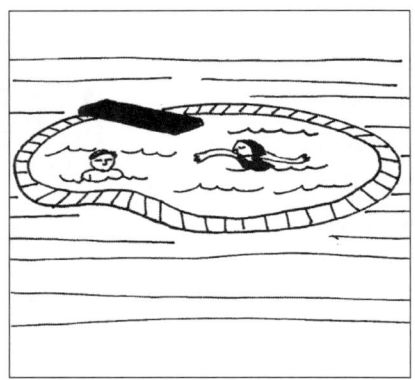

2

3

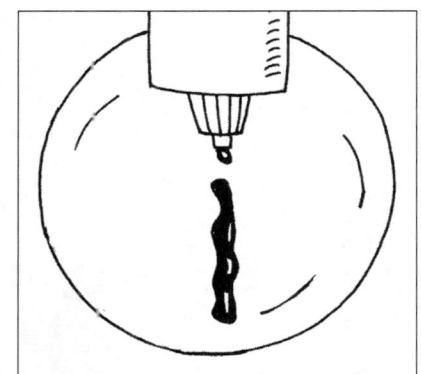  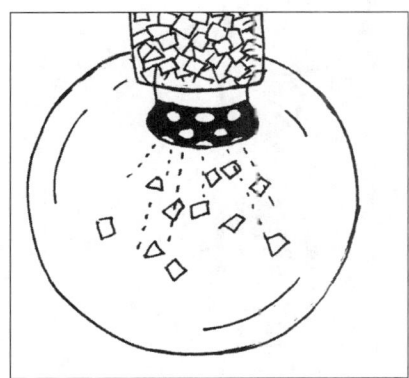

4

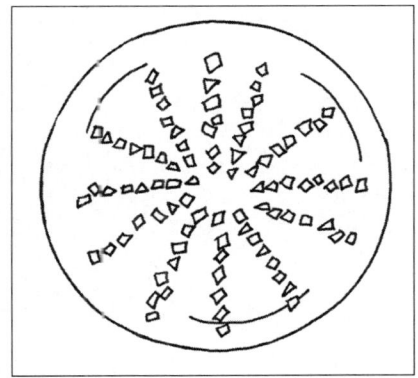 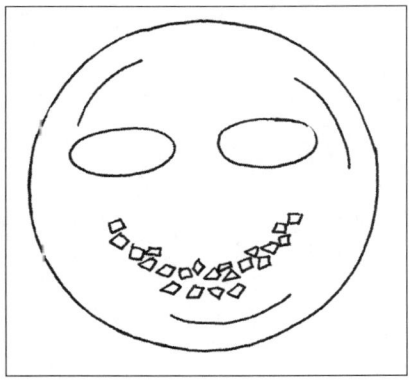 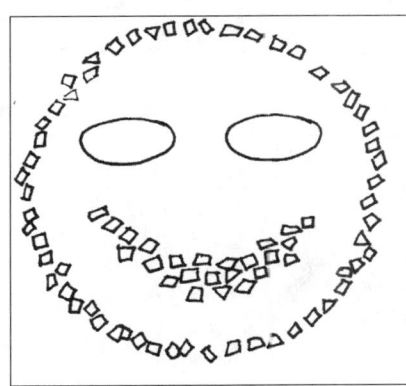

Name _____ Date _____

5

  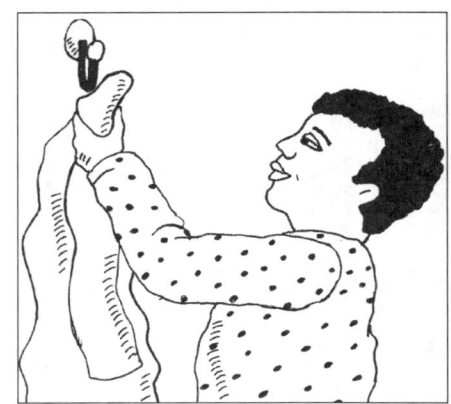

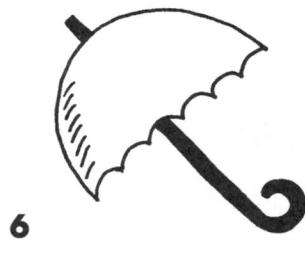

6

  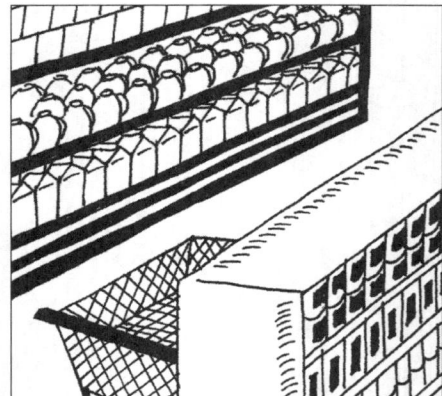

7

8

Name _____ Date _____

9

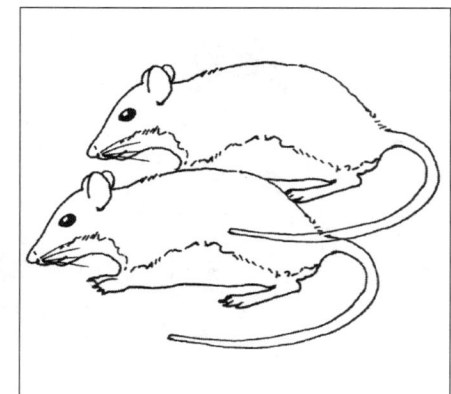

10

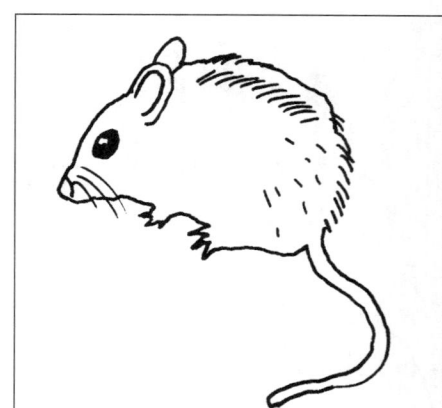

11

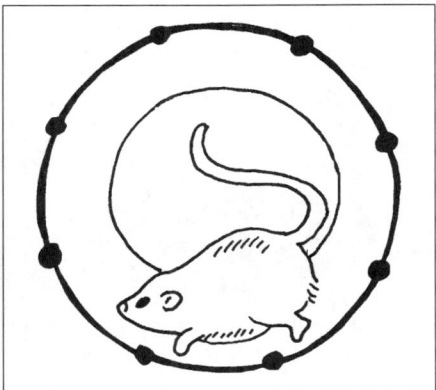

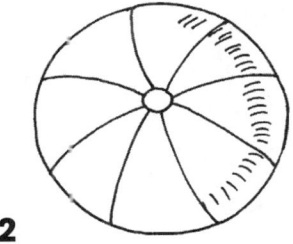

12

Name _____ Date _____

13

14

 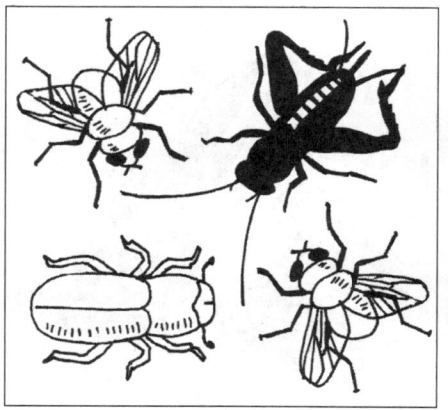 

15

16

  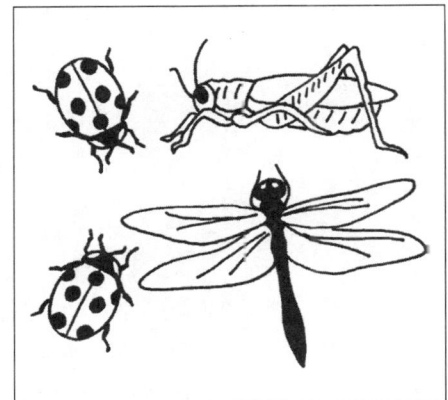

Individual Pretest Scoring Chart

Student Name _____ Date _____

Teacher Name _____ Grade _____

Skill Cluster Comprehension or Word Study Strategy	Item Numbers	Midyear Score
1 Literary Elements Analyze Character Analyze Story Elements	2, 6, 7, 8	/4
2 Relating Ideas Compare and Contrast Identify Cause and Effect Identify Sequence of Events	3, 11, 13, 14	/4
3 Inferences and Conclusions Draw Conclusions Make Inferences Make Predictions	1, 5, 12, 15	/4
4 Distinguishing Important Information Identify Main Idea and Supporting Details Summarize Information	4, 9, 10, 16	/4
Total		/16
Percent Score		___%

Individual Midyear Test Scoring Chart

Student Name _____ Date _____

Teacher Name _____ Grade _____

Skill Cluster Comprehension or Word Study Strategy	Item Numbers	Posttest Score
1 **Literary Elements** Analyze Character Analyze Story Elements	2, 6, 7, 8	/4
2 **Relating Ideas** Compare and Contrast Identify Cause and Effect Identify Sequence of Events	3, 11, 13, 14	/4
3 **Inferences and Conclusions** Draw Conclusions Make Inferences Make Predictions	1, 5, 12, 15	/4
4 **Distinguishing Important Information** Identify Main Idea and Supporting Details Summarize Information	4, 9, 10, 16	/4
Total		/16
Percent Score		___%

Individual Posttest Scoring Chart

Student Name _____ Date _____

Teacher Name _____ Grade _____

Skill Cluster Comprehension or Word Study Strategy	Item Numbers	Midyear Score
1 **Literary Elements** Analyze Character Analyze Story Elements	2, 6, 7, 8	/4
2 **Relating Ideas** Compare and Contrast Identify Cause and Effect Identify Sequence of Events	3, 11, 13, 14	/4
3 **Inferences and Conclusions** Draw Conclusions Make Inferences Make Predictions	1, 5, 12, 15	/4
4 **Distinguishing Important Information** Identify Main Idea and Supporting Details Summarize Information	4, 9, 10, 16	/4
Total		/16
Percent Score		___%

Teacher Name _____ Grade _____

Student Name	Pretest		Midyear Test		Posttest	
	Total Correct	Percent Score	Total Correct	Percent Score	Total Correct	Percent Score

Student Name _____ Date _____

Teacher Name _____ Grade _____

No.	Comprehension or Word Study Strategy	Reading or Listening		Reading or Listening	
		Date of 1st Assessment	Score	Date of 2nd Assessment	Score
1–2	Analyze Character				
3–4	Analyze Story Elements				
5–6	Compare and Contrast				
7–8	Draw Conclusions				
9–10	Identify Main Idea and Supporting Details				
11–12	Identify Cause and Effect				
13–14	Identify Sequence of Events				
15–16	Make Inferences				
17–18	Make Predictions				
19–20	Summarize Information				

Common Core State Standards and Virginia SOL Correlations

Pretest			Midyear Test			Posttest		
Item	**CCSS**	**VA SOL**	**Item**	**CCSS**	**VA SOL**	**Item**	**CCSS**	**VA SOL**
1.	RL.K.1	K.9c	1.	RL.K.1	K.9c	1.	RL.K.1	K.9c
2.	RL.K.3	K.9g	2.	RL.K.3	K.9g	2.	RL.K.3	K.9g
3.	RI.K.3	K.10 CF	3.	RI.K.3	K.10 CF	3.	RI.K.3	K.10 CF
4.	RI.K.2	K.10 CF	4.	RI.K.2	K.10 CF	4.	RI.K.2	K.10 CF
5.	RL.K.1	K.9c	5.	RL.K.1	K.9c	5.	RL.K.1	K.9c
6.	RL.K.3	K.9d	6.	RL.K.3	K.9d	6.	RL.K.3	K.9d
7.	RL.K.3	K.9d	7.	RL.K.3	K.9d	7.	RL.K.3	K.9d
8.	RL.K.3	K.9g	8.	RL.K.3	K.9g	8.	RL.K.3	K.9g
9	RI.K.2	K.10a	9	RI.K.2	K.10a	9	RI.K.2	K.10a
10	RI.K.2	K.10 CF	10	RI.K.2	K.10 CF	10	RI.K.2	K.10 CF
11.	RI.K.1	K.10 CF	11.	RI.K.1	K.10 CF	11.	RI.K.1	K.10 CF
12.	RI.K.1	K.10a	12.	RI.K.1	K.10a	12.	RI.K.1	K.10a
13.	RI.K.3	K.10 CF	13.	RI.K.3	K.10 CF	13.	RI.K.3	K.10 CF
14.	RI.K.3	K.10 CF	14.	RI.K.3	K.10 CF	14.	RI.K.3	K.10 CF
15.	RI.K.1	K.10 CF	15.	RI.K.1	K.10 CF	15.	RI.K.1	K.10 CF
16.	RI.K.2	K.10a	16.	RI.K.2	K.10a	16.	RI.K.2	K.10a

Notes